My Breath Loves Me

Claire E. Hallinan

ISBN 978-1-7330356-2-0

For Grandma Masu

The breath is a gift given when we are born.

It's okay to be angry.
When my friend jumps in line ahead of me,
I am angry.

Instead of saying with a mean voice
and a mad face, "Don't cut,"
Take a deep breath into your tummy and
out to the world.

You might notice
your fists are clenched into balls,
your heart is beating fast,
and your lips are tight.
Just say to yourself, "I feel angry."

Count your breaths slowly.
One breathing in, two breathing out,
three in, and four out.

Now you might notice
your own breaths are normal.
Keep breathing.

Then, ask your friend with a kind voice,
"Did you notice I was here before you?"

Chances are, he will say,
"I am sorry, I didn't know."

When I am understood, I feel peaceful.

It's okay to be sad.
When my friend ignores me and
runs off during recess,
I am sad.

Instead of whining or tattletaling,
Take a deep breath,
reach your hands up towards the sky
while you breathe in,
and reach down towards the ground
as you breathe out.

You might notice your throat is choked up,
your mouth turns down to a frown,
and your eyes are wet.
Just say to yourself, "I feel sad."

Breathe with your arms.
Breathe in as you open your arms,
breathe out and hug yourself.
Breathe in and open your arms,
breathe out and hug yourself.

Now you might notice
your breaths love you.
Keep breathing.

Then, look around the playground
for people you haven't played with
in a while.

When I can talk to new friends,
I feel courageous.
When I play with my new friends,
I feel happy.

It's okay to be jealous.
When my teacher compliments
my friend, I feel jealous.

Instead of saying, "I don't care anyway,"
Take a deep breath
into the top of your shoulders and
out to your fingers.

You might notice your chest is tight,
your fingers are tingling,
and your stomach is churning.
Just say to yourself, "I feel jealous."

Cup your hands in front of your heart.
Breathe in and
open your hands like a flower,
breathe out and close your hands.
Breathe in to bloom, breathe out to close.

Now you might notice
your breaths want to connect with you.
Keep breathing.

Then, bravely congratulate your friend,
"Good job, buddy!"

Chances are, he will say,
"Thank you! You'll be next!"
When I am recognized, I feel content.

Breathing helps me notice my feelings,
Breathing helps me notice
my body's sensations,
Breathing helps me calm down,
Breathing helps me show my compassion.

When I respond kindly, my friends smile.
When I see their smiles, I feel hopeful.

It's always okay to be kind.
When I help my friend pick up her crayons,
I feel kind.

Instead of letting it go so quickly,
Just say to yourself, "I am kind,"
And take a big breath.

You might notice
your cheeks are moving up,
your heart is warm,
and your body is relaxed.

Keep breathing.
You will find lots of smiles in your life.

The breath is a gift given
when we are born.
When we notice it and
learn how to live with it,
We will feel full of gratitude.
Be curious and
be friends with your breath.
Our lives are meant to be filled with
peace and happiness.

ABOUT THE AUTHOR

Claire E. Hallinan, MAEd, was born in Japan and lives with her family in Washington. Claire has a passion for making sense of the world, building relationships, and inspiring others to find themselves in happiness. She is a writer, an entrepreneur, a mindfulness practitioner, and a National Board Certified Teacher. Her memoir, *Gift of Gratitude*, and building relationship book, *I Notice*, are available on Amazon.

Contact Claire E. Hallinan at claire.e.hallinan@gmail.com.

CPSIA information can be obtained
at www.ICGtesting.com
Printed in the USA
LVHW070510200723
752876LV00045B/354